Kurt Luchs

The Sound of One Hand Slapping

SV

SurVision Books

First published in 2022 by
SurVision Books
Dublin, Ireland
Reggio di Calabria, Italy
www.survisionmagazine.com

Copyright © Kurt Luchs, 2022
Cover image © Anatoly Kudryavitsky, 2022
Design © SurVision Books, 2022

ISBN: 978-1-912963-33-1

This book is in copyright. No part of this publication may be reproduced, stored in a retrieval system, or transmitted in any form or by any means without the prior permission in writing from the publisher.

Acknowledgments

Grateful acknowledgment is made to the editors of the following, in which some of these poems, or versions of them, originally appeared:

The American Journal of Poetry: "Socrates"
Bacopa Literary Review: "The Music of the Words"
Die Leere Mitte: "Family Metaphors"
Doubly Mad Journal: "Apology"
Hawaii Pacific Review: "A Real Question with No Real Answers"
The Hollins Critic: "First and Last"
Innisfree Poetry Journal: "Beginning Near the End"
JMWW: "Sudden Silence"
London Grip: "Love Poem to My Love Poems," "Another Minor Poet"
MacQueen's Quinterly: "Lives of the Gods"
MockingHeart Review: "Dehydrated Tree Frog"
MONO: "The Eighties," "Observation Bias"
The Nonconformist: "Secret Messages"
The Opiate: "Flattened," "Baked"
Paper Dragon: "Migration"
pioneertown: "Always Be Closing"
Sonder Magazine: "Stage Five"
Steam Ticket: "World Records"
Two Thirds North: "I'm Ready"
Verse-Virtual: "Painted Turtle"

CONTENTS

Beginning Near the End	5
Love Poem to My Love Poems	6
Sudden Silence	8
Migration	10
Dehydrated Tree Frog	11
The Eighties	12
Flattened	14
The Music of the Words	15
Family Metaphors	16
World Records	17
Apology	18
A Real Question with No Real Answers	20
Observation Bias	22
Stage Five	24
Socrates	26
Baked	28
Acid	30
Lives of the Gods	32
Secret Messages	33
Painted Turtle	34
Always Be Closing	35
Another Minor Poet	36
My Dream	37
I'm Ready	38
First and Last	40

Beginning Near the End

The waitress could spot a first date
that was going well, they can always tell.
I finished your salad. You finished my sentences.
We both got tipsy, but not with wine.
Incipient joy can have a similar effect
and can also make you descend the stairs
unsteadily, the same way the sun was going down,
one hand on a bannister of clouds.
Back at your house your rescue dog got out
and had to be rescued all over again,
a furry parable from a parallel universe
that was not lost on me.
Our hands found each other, then our mouths,
and the conversation continued,
even better without words.
On the long drive home my heart raced
faster than my car, and the thunderhead clouds
floating on the horizon flashed with heat lightning,
silent fireworks lit from top to bottom,
the summer sky electrified repeatedly.

Love Poem to My Love Poems

(after "Poem to Some of My Recent Poems" by James Tate)

Honestly, most of you are better than what you try so hard
to celebrate. Not that you have given Shakespeare's bones
any reason to quiver with envy in their dark eternal nest,
but you are manifestly superior to any song by Air Supply.
Somewhere in that amorphous vacant lot
between immortality and mediocrity
is where you little lichens cling to the cracked stone
that is my life. Some of you are phosphorescent
and glow occasionally, others pulse with a primitive beat
in the blood that is either very bad jazz
or very good rock and roll. One of you repented
and joined a speechless monastery where the only poetry
allowed is the bell tolling for the noonday meal.
Another decided to become a policeman, who when called
to a domestic dispute automatically shoots to kill
both parties as a matter of general principle.
Justifiable romanticide, they call it.
There are so many ways to go wrong in this world,
so few to go right, it's a wonder any of you turned out at all.
While I am your only father, you have many mothers,
all of them desirable at one point
and leaving something to be desired at another.

I hope you never lose touch with each other
because aside from your raggedy brothers and sisters
you are completely alone. Nobody cares
about anyone else's love or the stray
bastard utterance to which it may have given birth.

Sudden Silence

(for Adam Zagajewski, 1945–2021)

A certain music has stopped.
As when the voice of a bird
calling from a lone tree
grows suddenly silent
the moment you draw near.
We won't have that tune again
except in books, where music goes to die
or sometimes to live.
I think yours will live
after a hush in the pine forest
and a pause and many tears.

A certain music has stopped.
A music notable for daring to be uncertain
during an age of official certitudes
when any question, however tentative,
was a political act.
In this as in a multitude of things
you were the father I would have preferred,
the older brother I never had,
the professor whose master class I did not take
but from which I learned anyway, stealing whatever I could.

A certain music has stopped.
You grew up amid rubble both physical and metaphysical,
which must be how you learned that a broken thing
can still be beautiful, like the human spirit
or the collapsing cathedral we call civilization.
For me and countless others
you became the reluctant choir leader
stubbornly continuing to sing in the ruins.

A certain music has stopped.
And perhaps now would be the time
to remember that music is also
the space between the notes,
the little silences that give meaning
to the greater silence,
the music that does not stop.

Migration

The giant spiders are migrating again.
Their journey is long and perilous
because they can only travel in nightmares.
Last night as I dozed fitfully, two of them
came down the hill, and when they turned off Red Wing Avenue
I was able to blow out some of their dark, bulbous eyes
before the shotgun became black smoke rising from my hands
and a pterodactyl in a bus driver's cap
lifted me screaming into the sky.
Today, as I go about my business—
stamping ALREADY PAID on all of my overdue bills—
I can feel that it is they who sleep uneasily,
relishing yet also fearing our next encounter,
their jaws grinding, their unbearably hairy legs
twitching in anticipation.
This time there will be two shotguns
and a phosphorous grenade, and if all else fails,
a club wrapped in barbed wire at the big end.
Let your remaining eyes look upon that
and tremble, my dreamy darlings...

Dehydrated Tree Frog

Half-brown, half-green, half-grown and half-alive now, he must have
found his way, or lost his way, into the apartment garage,
a smooth pond of concrete into which he could not dive.
There are a few things to eat here if he could overpower them,
but nothing to drink or bathe in, and this miniscule creature
was made to live where the water meets the land,
halfway between us and the fishes.
(Maybe he's a she. How would I know?)
It can't have been more than an hour or two since his deadly mistake,
and already he's dusty, slow and shriveling,
unable to evade my hand. In most parts of the globe
the humans would consider him a delicacy.
Here he is simply a fellow traveler in need of help.
I cradle him in my palm and tip him gently
into the car's drink cozy. At the bottom of the winding drive
I stop, step to the curb, and pour him into the dewy grass,
there being no other moisture nearby, and him so close to gone.
I don't stay to watch the result, preferring to hope for the best
for this profligate, persistent, perversely persevering thing called life.

The Eighties

The usual group had gathered at the usual time and place
for breakfast, had ordered and eaten the usual dishes,
and had run the usual topics of conversation into the ground.
Why was the whole world crashing around our heads?
Where would it all end? How could the two halves of the
country keep from killing each other and get anything useful
accomplished? Everyone else had paid and left, but I just
sat there, staring into space and holding Sheryl's hand in mine.
"Shall we?" she said. "No, we shall not. Can you hear that?"
I said. "Hear what?" she said, frowning. "That song," I said,
pointing to the loudspeaker in the ceiling. "What about it?
What is it?" she said. "I don't know what it is, they aren't
playing it loud enough to make out the lyrics," I said,
"but I can tell you when it was produced: The Eighties."
She said, "How do you know that? And what difference
does it make?" "That echoing electronic drum sound high
in the mix, those cheesy synthesizers, and worst of all
that superfluous saxophone solo, could not have come
from any other decade," I said. "I can't hear the words,"
she said. "The words don't matter," I said. "They could be
telling us we don't need another hero, or that our whisper
is careless, or to harden our hearts. What matters is a sound
so dull, so pointless and unthinking, that it was dead before
the sun went down on the day it was born. That sound caused
music fans to turn on each other with unbelievable savagery.

There were riots, assaults, murders, people burned alive. A new book just came out proving that most saxophone players were quietly rounded up toward the end of the decade and put into secret death camps for orderly disposal." "Oh," she said. "Well, I kind of like Eighties music." "Me too," I said. "The Eighties are the best."

Flattened

Coming out of the breakfast restaurant and heading toward my car
I step over what I think is an autumn leaf,
brownish-green edged with red, and realize
it's a flattened frog floating on a still lake of asphalt.
If this were an episode of *CSI: Frogtown*
it could be determined that he made one proud leap off the curb
before being turned into an amphibian pancake
by a hit-and-run inflatable tire.
Who do I call? Who do I get in touch with?
Is there a Mrs. Frog in the marsh down the hill,
hiding among the cattails and waiting for her little man
to come home? She'll be waiting a long time.
Are there tadpoles who just became orphans?
They're America's problem now, but America has enough problems,
beset as she is on all sides by those two implacables,
death and eternity. As with almost everything else that gives me pause,
there is nothing to be done, so nothing is what I do,
very carefully, looking both ways as I cross to my car.

The Music of the Words

Our mother would recite Yeats,
Frost, Dylan Thomas and Shakespeare
while doing housework or cooking,
she was a terrible housekeeper
and her cooking was one step removed
from negligent homicide,
but she had a lovely voice
which made the words sing
with a hey nonny nonny
and a permanent case
of postpartum depression.
Sometimes she switched to ballads
made popular among American folkies
by the Clancy Brothers,
Pete Seeger and Joan Baez.
Either way the music of the words
sunk in deep, the difference between
conversation and verse
was not lost in translation,
the rhythms and rhymes
made it all stick
and we learned that poetry
is simply part of life
like sweeping the floor badly
or burning the toast in tune.

Family Metaphors

Our household was a novel inside a play,
the novel being *Lord of the Flies*
and the play being *Who's Afraid of Virginia Woolf?*
Seven feral children shipwrecked on the reef of a bad marriage
made a savage society of their own devices,
a tribe doomed to wander the deserted suburban island
on which they found themselves stranded.
Their double sentence: life without parole, death by madness.
Seven bodies survived, seven sarcophagi
filled with psyches crushed to dust.
Did you know that in the netherworld the dead eat their own,
there being nothing else? And then they are all
eaten by sand and waves and wind and time.
It's another story without a happy ending,
a story with the single lonely virtue of being true.

World Records

The loudest bird call ever recorded was made
by a male white bellbird, whose mating cry
can reach 125 decibels even when the female
is already right next to him, a phenomenon
previously observed only at office Christmas parties.
The former record holder was the screaming piha
at 116 decibels. (Note to self: remember
to rename my punk group the Screaming Pihas.)
I prefer quieter birds myself, like the turkey vulture
who's been circling me for three days,
looking for any sign of weakness, his shadow
crisscrossing my deck again and again.
About his personal life I know nothing,
but I can tell you what he wants for dinner.
And honestly, he's welcome to nibble on my carcass
as long as he doesn't start until sometime after death.
Just now I am in the process of perfecting my own mating cry,
a kind of refined whimper that ends with a sob
and goes well with a glass of red wine sipped in solitude.
My cry cannot begin to compete with the screaming piha,
let alone the white bellbird, and is mercifully
inaudible to human females even when they are already
right next to me. Clearly, I and my kind
are not long for this world,
and as the turkey vulture's patient shadow reminds me,
Darwin's great work must go on.

Apology

May I speak freely?
Thank you. That makes it easier.
How disappointed you must be,
sitting there expecting something more,
an insight or two, a scrap of wisdom,
a bit of beauty dressed up in rhyme
or alliteration or the dazzling lies of metaphor.
Unfortunately, this is all I have for you.
We woke up in the same unfurnished apartment
chained to the same radiator
by the same absentee landlord
who has never once shown his face.
Occasionally food and drink appear,
occasionally a bucket.
When we tire of screaming our fool heads off
there follows the delightful contrast of silence
which always feels as if
it's about to say something, but never does.
And that is a statement in itself I suppose.
Why do we scream?
He's been getting away with it for billions of years.
There is no chance of him
being brought to justice anytime soon.
The changing seasons, the few square inches
of sky and cloud we can see through the window

leave you mute but make me want to sing.
It takes all kinds to make a world,
even such a world as this.
If only my song brought comfort to one of us,
like the shadow of the tree
that crosses the wall each day,
slowly lengthening, almost as if
the tree were growing, almost
as if it were really there.
Perhaps it is. Most likely we'll never know.
We lie down with illusion
and wake up with mystery,
born in chains, dying in chains,
my song the only thing that ever escapes,
that can come and go as it pleases.
I'm so sorry.

A Real Question with No Real Answers

What is hope?
A moss that grows
silent and unseen
on any surface,
a light that becomes visible
only after your eyes
have adjusted to the darkness,
a note that hangs in the air
after the bird has flown,
a green shoot erupting
from a dead stump.

Sworn enemy of reason,
dubious friend of life,
estranged cousin of death,
confounder of statistics,
historians and tax collectors.

When you talk to yourself
she's listening,
without a word
but holding your hand
and gazing over your shoulder
at a future
that might still be.

She sees what has not
quite come to pass
and perhaps never will,
the path un-walked,
and yet—this is confusing—
she remains blind and deaf
to whatever would be
unhelpful to perceive,
her every affirmation
contains a denial.

She scratches the face
of disaster and carries
a mustard seed
under one fingernail.

Observation Bias

They had me in the observation ward, no doubt the better
to observe me. They had their reasons. In the previous week
my body had started to grow feathers, my hair had fallen out
and my newly bald head was sprouting something that looked like
a rooster's comb. I was neither proud nor ashamed of these
developments. This was simply my new reality. Each morning,
noon and evening the doctors would poke me, prod me,
take my temperature, attach me to various electronic instruments
and record their findings on their tablets, clucking with consternation.
One day a doctor said that my beak was coming along just fine.
I started to say, "What beak?" but then touched my nose
and realized he was right. Instead I asked if he had any seed corn.
I reached through the bars of my cage—that's what it was, really—
imploring him to find me some harder, more solid food.
He looked at me with revulsion and said, "Don't you dare
touch me you filthy creature!" Then he ordered me to move
to the other end of the cage, the one labeled "Observation Bias."
On a table outside the cage were several painful and injurious
but nonlethal weapons: pea shooters, sling shots, an air rifle,
and a professional-grade baseball. First he shot me with each
shooting weapon, and then he threw a fastball right at my head.
The baseball beaned me and knocked me off my feet. "You're
out!" he said. "And let that be a lesson to you." Nor was the
physical hurt the worst of it. I won't even repeat what he said

about my place in the new pecking order. I pretended to cower in a corner of the cage, fluttering and squawking, but already I was beginning to compose my Oscar-winning screenplay, *Revenge of the Man-Chicken*.

Stage Five

As soon as Dr. Kvachkov ushered me into his office
and closed the door, I realized the news was not good.
"I'm afraid your test results leave no room for doubt," he said.
"Cancer?" I said. He nodded grimly. "How bad is it?" I said.
"As bad as can be," he said. "Stage five." I sat there stunned
for a moment. I said, "I didn't even know there was a stage five."
"The existence of stage five is the most closely guarded secret
in the world," he said. "Stage four is terminal," I said.
"How am I still alive?" Dr. Kvachkov paused and said,
"That's the hell of it. You're not." I gaped at him, open-mouthed,
unable to speak. "I won't pretend we understand it," he said,
"because we don't. It seems that muscle memory and habit
are even stronger than death. As near as we can tell,
three percent of the world's population are in stage five,
and the number keeps growing. There are at least nine people
in Congress with this condition, along with some top CEO's
and several entire classic rock bands." "How long do I have, doc?"
I said. "That's anybody's guess," he said. "You might go on
as you are for another twenty years, or you might keel over
tomorrow." I said, "I have so many questions. For instance,
will my flesh start putrefying and sloughing off in handfuls?"
"Don't worry, I can give you a topical ointment for that," he said.
He scrawled something on his prescription pad and handed
it to me. I said, "Another thing that's troubling me is,
should I tell my wife?" The doctor looked at me and sighed.

"I guess it's all right to let you know now," he said. "She's been in stage five since the second Reagan administration."
There was nothing more to say. I stood up on my two dead legs and silently commanded my animated corpse to leave his office. It's funny, when the worst happens, it's never quite as bad as you feared. For a man who had just learned he's way beyond doomed, I felt surprisingly buoyant. Maybe stage five is the silver lining we've all been looking for, I thought. Outside the sun was shining. It was a beautiful day. The sidewalk was crowded with happy people doing happy things.
And just think: three out of every hundred were as dead as last week's pizza, part of a clandestine club that included me. How thrilling! I searched their eyes, looking for the secret sign.

Socrates

Almost every dialogue follows the same pattern.
Socrates is talking to a businessman,
or a soldier, or a politician, or one of the idle rich
who has time for these word games.
All he does is ask questions.
Seemingly innocent questions, like a detective
with the endless patience of the police laying a trap:
What is virtue? Why are we here?
Is there a righteous form of government?
Whatever the topic, the poor fellow starts
by confidently mouthing the current platitudes
but Socrates will have none of it.
Question follows question with the ruthless precision of chess
until every comforting illusion has been stripped away,
every pretense of knowledge, and the other person in the dialogue
has been shown to be as ignorant as the day he was born.
The reader can be pardoned for concluding
Socrates is an asshole, just as the Greek rulers did.
I used to think that. Now I think
he's the kindest person who ever lived.
Life is so precarious, so short.
We enter it with nothing, we leave the same way.
We cannot improve on the poverty of existence
except with wisdom, and there is no room for wisdom
in a mind that thinks it already knows something.

These days I find I have been permanently infected
with the philosopher's questions, I cheer him on
in every dialogue, and as he raises his glass
of hemlock, I raise mine too,
the house serving no other beverage, and I discover peace
in admitting I know nothing, I never did.

Baked

There are worse ways to enter the workforce
than by washing dishes in a bakery.
After cleaning a hundred angel food cake pans in a day,
doing the dishes at home will never again
feel like a chore. Piece of cake!

Once or twice an hour the counter girls
would step from the shop into the back room
to have a cigarette and bare their breasts at us
by the dim red light of the ovens,
as if unveiling two more fresh loaves.

This was back when employee morale
used to mean something.
Certainly it caused me to scrub more furiously.
Cyd was in love with me but I was in love
with Jennie, a triangle no geometry could ever resolve.

Those of us in the back would also sometimes
pause to peer through the blinds at the parade of humanity
in the shop, including local celebrities like the mayor
and Ringmaster Ned from *Bozo's Circus*
who needed his prune kolaches every Friday.

Mr. Belushi came by several times a week
but no one knew who his sons were yet,
so to us he was just another crazy Albanian.
The real fun began every evening after the shop closed
and the Pennsylvania Dutch couple who owned the place

climbed upstairs to their second-floor apartment.
The rest of us would share a joint
lit in the glow of the ovens and have food fights
with handfuls of whipped cream
and lard scooped out of giant tubs.

Afterward we would carefully put everything
back in its place, because waste is a sin.
I was not able to eat baked goods for the next decade,
and to this day the smell of warm bread
arouses me in a way I can't begin to explain.

Acid

Nothing happens at first.
Just for emphasis, it happens again.
Then I notice that the lines of my bedroom
are no longer straight but wriggling, alive,
trying to crawl away, everything is alive except
the transistor radio, which has gone
suddenly silent, the music deciding
to come out of a Veteran's Day poppy instead.
I don't remember stepping outside
but here I am. The moon has become
a silver sun wreathed with electric ghosts,
the night is breathing, and not in time
with my own breath or my heart.
Two seagulls that are not here
are tearing at the flesh of a giant
morning glory, also imaginary,
yet with a heartbreakingly realistic face
and a mouth making an anguished "O."
The screams of the birds and the flower
seem to be coming from far away
like the wind that blots out whatever it touches.
A man in a black windbreaker approaches
to say that he is second-shift me
and I can go home now. So I do,

in the blink of a dilated eye, and now
I'm holding the radio to my ear
awaiting further instructions in the endless
spaces between bursts of static.

Lives of the Gods

As I passed by the bakery downtown, inhaling the many delicious
scents emanating from within, a man stepped from the shadows
and asked me if I had any spare change. "Honestly, I don't,"
I said. "I never carry coins, and the only bills I have in my
wallet are tens and twenties. "I'll take one of those," he said.
"I'm sure you would," I said, "but not today I'm afraid."
He said, "You should be afraid. I could obliterate you with a wave
of my hand. I am a god in human form. My name is Ogmar the
Terrible." I shook his obliterating hand. "Nice to meet you, Ogmar,"
I said. "I too am a god. You can call me Phil the Mildly Asthmatic.
The thing is, Ogmar, while I don't have many religious scruples,
one of them is that I never make offerings to gods whose names
include the word 'terrible.' That's sort of a nonnegotiable for me."
He looked perplexed, then his grimy face brightened and he said,
"For you I could be Ogmar the Kind. Gods can do that. I could
start by breaking one of those tens for you at the bakery."
"Your divinity is becoming more apparent to me by the second,"
I said, pulling out a ten and handing it to him. "Keep the change,
Ogmar." "Oh thank you, mighty and wise Phil," he said.
I continued down the street, hoping to find a drugstore that sold
god-sized doses of anti-inflammatories.

Secret Messages

Life is a record album I sometimes listen to backward
searching for secret messages,
though the ones I hear playing it forward the usual way
are no less mysterious.
Just now, for example, I notice a spider
has claimed a corner of the ceiling
where three straight lines converge
as in a painting by Mondrian,
only at the center of this composition is murder
if you happen to be a fly or a moth.
Does death really have to be in the middle of a thing
before we can call it beautiful?
Earlier today I was listening to Simon and Garfunkel
singing, "Save the Life of My Child,"
a song I've known all my life, about a boy leaping
to his doom from a New York building,
and for the first time I heard the words
"Hello darkness my old friend"
inserted from an older song, slowed down
and buried in the mix so as to be almost unrecognizable.
Yet there it was, a secret message hiding in plain sight,
waiting all these years for me to finally pay attention.

Painted Turtle

Hey watch this
said one of the older kids.

We had been kicking stones
and he lifted one over his head
and blithely hurled it
at a painted turtle floating in the lagoon.
The turtle ducked, but too late;
its shell exploded like a paper bag.

Crap, I hope I didn't throw my arm out
he commented.
That sure was something, huh?

I looked at the stones near my feet
and then at him, sizing him up.
Yep, it sure was
I said.

Always Be Closing

The company is constantly springing the latest sales training on us, just trying to help I suppose. Now Brigette and I were in front of a potential customer, putting some of the new techniques into practice. She sweetly asked the guy, whose name was Pete, for a glass of water. Then she stood up and poured it slowly over her head with one hand while rubbing her stomach with the other and saying, "Glug, glug, glug!" That certainly got Pete's attention. He stared at her, fascinated, as she pulled a medium-sized halibut from her purse and smacked herself in the face with it, once on each cheek. She held the fish up, gazing into its dead eyes, and said, "You've been a very bad boy." Then she threw it with all her might at the conference room window, which shattered instantly, spraying us with shards of glass. Pete grinned from ear to ear and nodded his head while he brushed glass from his sweater. "I think I see what you mean," he said. "You don't see anything, monkey boy," said Brigette. She took off her blazer and gave it to me to hold. Then she leaped across the table, grabbed Pete by the throat and sucker punched him in the stomach. He bent over, gasping, and said, "That's the most convincing presentation I've ever seen. Consider me sold." Brigette walked around the table, took the blazer from me, put it back on, straightened her glasses and sat down. "How many color copiers would you like, Mr. Drummond?" she said.

Another Minor Poet

(after "A Minor Poet" by Jorge Luis Borges)

The song I hope to sing is one
where the words march into the whiteness of the page
like Captain Robert Falcon Scott trudging toward the South Pole,
fated to arrive five weeks after Amundsen,
that damned Norwegian upstart, and even worse,
doomed to die on the return journey,
braving the vast Antarctic icebox again at forty below.

There is no shame in being the second man
to reach the Pole or walk on the Moon (who was that again?),
no dishonor in being the first forgotten,
snow-blind, descending into darkness by means of the light.
The sweet amnesia of snow and cold is no less merciful
than that of the poem never written, never published,
or perhaps, published and quickly lost among so many others.
Though we appear to be hurtling away from each other
we are all on the same journey,
unknowingly following imaginary, invisible longitudinal lines
that must meet in the long night at the wrong end of Earth.

My Dream

The simple, honest people of my little town
form a circle and put me in the middle of it.
They begin to pelt me with copies
of *The Lottery and Other Stories* by Shirley Jackson,
first the paperback, which gives me minor welts and bruises
and yes, paper cuts, and then the hardcover,
which does more serious damage,
breaking my nose, taking out one eye,
then the other, causing a concussion
and eventually both a heart attack and a stroke.
As I lay dying, with a completely unintentional
and irrelevant Faulkner reference,
I thought I heard a mother scold a child
for accidentally throwing a copy
of *The Haunting of Hill House*. Or was that
a dream within the dream?
No matter. I was happy to have been a live human
for a few decades, and even happier now
to be a dead metaphor.

I'm Ready

Not that I'm looking to go
any time soon, mind you,
but if death should take me now
I would not feel cheated.
I've tasted everything this life
can offer: love, true and false,
hate, always true (why is it
hate that's always true?),
the quarter moon a slice of blood orange
just above the horizon,
the sun at twilight a tulip dipped in lava,
the music of Bach
which by itself justifies
all the failings of humanity,
the bittersweet joy of fatherhood—
helping a soul to grow
even as she grows away from you...
Yes, I've seen it all:
two giant snapping turtles making love
very carefully, as they say,
a redwood tree that wears a cloud
for a hat,
a Dutch still life
more beautiful than any real fruit,
and a heart that beats only for me

day and night.
Whatever the foreshortened future may hold
it can't surpass any of these,
so to echo my beloved Bach,
"Come, sweetest death."
I'm ready.
Just not quite yet,
if it's all the same to you.
I want to spend some time
with that beating heart.

First and Last

The first rays of dawn shot slantwise
through the blinds. I stirred
and rolled over to face death
staring at me in her quiet way
which I have come to admire.
A clumsier companion would have blurted out,
"I love to watch you sleep,"
but with us there is no need for words.
I have no idea what she is thinking
and that is the beauty of it.
Love requires mystery and surrender.
Between us we have both.
When the unheralded moment arrives
my capitulation will be unilateral
and her conquest of my being complete.
Then I will know, if I have time to reflect,
whether her final gift is a bullet,
a head-on collision in the night,
or the slow, halting waltz of neurological decay.
For now we sip coffee from the same cup,
as close as two creatures can be,
watching the sunrise together,
and only one of us knows
whether it's the last.

Selected Poetry Titles Published by SurVision Books

Seeds of Gravity: An Anthology of Contemporary Surrealist Poetry from Ireland
Edited by Anatoly Kudryavitsky
ISBN 978-1-912963-18-8

Invasion: An Anthology of Ukrainian Poetry about the War
Edited by Tony Kitt
ISBN 978-1-912963-32-4

Noelle Kocot. *Humanity*
(New Poetics: USA)
ISBN 978-1-9995903-0-7

Marc Vincenz. *Einstein Fledermaus*
(New Poetics: USA)
ISBN 978-1-912963-20-1

Helen Ivory. *Maps of the Abandoned City*
(New Poetics: England)
ISBN 978-1-912963-04-1

Tony Kitt. *The Magic Phlute*
(New Poetics: Ireland)
ISBN 978-1-912963-08-9

Clayre Benzadón. *Liminal Zenith*
(New Poetics: USA)
ISBN 978-1-912963-11-9

Thomas Townsley. *Tangent of Ardency*
(New Poetics: USA)
ISBN 978-1-912963-15-7

Anton Yakovlev. *Chronos Dines Alone*
(Winner of James Tate Poetry Prize 2018)
ISBN 978-1-912963-01-0

Mikko Harvey & Jake Bauer. *Idaho Falls*
(Winner of James Tate Poetry Prize 2018)
ISBN 978-1-912963-02-7

John Bradley. *Spontaneous Mummification*
(Winner of James Tate Poetry Prize 2019)
ISBN 978-1-912963-13-3

John Thomas Allen. *Rolling in the Third Eye*
(Winner of James Tate Poetry Prize 2019)
ISBN 978-1-912963-15-7

Gary Glauber. *The Covalence of Equanimity*
(Winner of James Tate Poetry Prize 2019)
ISBN 978-1-912963-12-6

Charles Kell. *Pierre Mask*
(Winner of James Tate Poetry Prize 2019)
ISBN 978-1-912963-19-5

Charles Borkhuis. *Spontaneous Combustion*
(Winner of James Tate Poetry Prize 2021)
ISBN 978-1-912963-30-0

George Kalamaras. *That Moment of Wept*
ISBN 978-1-9995903-7-6

George Kalamaras. *Through the Silk-Heavy Rains*
ISBN 978-1-912963-28-7

Order our books from http://survisionmagazine.com/bookshop.htm

www.ingramcontent.com/pod-product-compliance
Lightning Source LLC
Chambersburg PA
CBHW071958060426
42444CB00043B/2566